THE SLOTH AND HER FRIENDS

HELP TRAIN YOUR CHILDREN'S IMAGINATION

Introduction

For many parents, curling up with a book for a bedtime story with their kid is a daily ritual. For others, it is the perfect time to spend time with their children after a busy day, and for some, it is something they should do but are not entirely sure why. Discover these benefits of bedtime stories for kids.

Sharpen their brains

Research shows that one of the greatest benefit of interacting with children, including reading to them stories, is that children learn a great deal of things- from improved logic skills to lowering their stress levels. Bedtime stories rewire the brain of a child and quicken their mastery of language. Their vocabulary repertoire is expanded and their listening and oral communication skills enhanced.

Enhance creativity and Stimulate imagination

If you are a good storyteller, then you should teleport your kid to a different realm- from reality to fantasy for the child to learn the difference between these two. This will enhance and stimulate his imagination.

Emotion development

The kid will learn to experience different emotions while empathizing with the characters of the story. The common emotions of sadness, happiness and anger may be encountered and he will learn to control these in real life.

Content

7 Tips to Help Ignite Your Child's Imagination

Imagination, often the concept we associate with joy, whimsy, and play, is just as easily involving cognitive capability, logical reasoning, and mental stability. The process the brain goes through when utilizing make-believe notions is a mixture of curiosity, adrenaline, and the practicing of creativity and exploration of different ideas previously unreached. Doing so exercises several parts of the adolescent mind, and will be reflected upon in the future, by means of open-mindedness, reason, and the ability to fathom abstractions above and beyond that of the average mind.

By incorporating these tips and activities into the lifestyles of both you and your child, your pudgy genius will not only be more mentally efficient, but happier and more capable overall.

1.   Ask Boggling Questions

Parents tend to underestimate the span of their child's intelligence, restraining their capacity. Ask questions that are "out of the box", for instance, "what do you think that toad is thinking?" or "how come the clouds are floating?" Questions that you wouldn't normally consider completely sane, probably absurd to the outside world, can be awe-inspiring and full of wonder to your child, opening doors of imagination and invention in their minds. In addition, try to respond to their answers with "why do you think that is?" or "how can you tell?", thereby teaching them that questions are meant to be explored, and ideas full of possibility. Most importantly, never allow your child to say "I don't know". Teach them that your questions have no right answer, as long as they make you think.

2.   Keep Questions Open-ended

Steer clear of words such as "wrong" or "try again", which will force children to believe that questions can only have one answer, with strict guidelines and a sole truth. They will later apply this mantra to their everyday behavior, and think in a more linear format, essentially restricting their minds and ideas.

3.   Ask "what if?"

What if trees could move? What if you your teacher were an ogre? What if giraffes could talk? Let your child explore things beyond the dimensions of reality, and allow them to conceive concepts far and wide.

4.   Tell Stories

Pictures and imagery are unimportant, even less effective than simply speaking a story to your child. Use different voices, adjectives, and hand gestures when speaking, allowing your child to fill in the blanks of the story, creating a sort of movie in their own heads. Unlike in TV, in stories, children do not have their visuals presented to them. Make these epic narratives engaging, and allow your child to add to the story. This will open the door to creative writing, as well as reading and extensive thought. It is so important to constantly exercise your child's mind, allowing it to be flexible and thrive in mentally straining instances in adulthood.

5.   Create Art

Allow your child to openly explore their artistic talent. By letting your child draw, paint, or simply create the ideas in their minds, you are solidifying the concepts they invent, giving them meaning and allowing them to come to life. Even if their drawing capabilities are short of Mozart material, by creating art, your child will learn to express his or herself, perhaps opening up new areas of interest.

You can create hand puppets, form houses out of old packing boxes, or have fun with finger paints. The expanse of art is endlessly vast, and it's fine simply to explore its plains.

6. Encourage Openness

In addition to openness regarding the imagination, encourage trying new things. Whether this is varying foods, different school clubs, and even new friendships, your child can experience anything from an engaging hobby to understanding the conditions of friendship. Moreover, try not to overly shelter your child. Children who understand death at an early age will better cope with it in the future, and adolescents familiar with financial instability will learn from their parent's experiences and be more understanding and compassionate toward adversity. Of course, there is a period in childhood when not to be too open, just keep in mind that hiding everything from your child is not realistic nor healthy.

7.   Leave Room for Growth

A flower doesn't bloom under watch, and a child's imagination cannot grow in a cramped environment. Allow him or her space to explore the world. Let your child establish independence, while still maintaining the assurance of an adult figure, in case things go astray. It's often hard to let go of your child, and that's OK, however it's imperative to refrain from being overly invasive, as this will likely cause your child to become dependent and create a barricade between them and their full capacity.

THE SLOTH AND HER FRIENDS

CHAPTER 1. The Lazy Sloths

The sloths' family lived in the forest. They loved to cling onto the branches of the trees and stay like that for weeks. Mother, father, Sister Lala and Brother Bala. They were very lazy, especially the mother, the father and Brother Bala. Sister Lala wasn't so lazy, but she behaved like the rest of her family because she thought that it was the right thing to do. Sister Lala looked around, saw that her parents and Brother Bala were resting in the sun and said:

"Mommy, daddy, Brother Bala, why are we always so motionless?" she asked.

There was silence. Apparently the sloths were too lazy to answer her.

"Why aren't we ever moving our bodies, mommy?" she asked her mother.

Very slowly, her mother opened her mouth to respond. It took a few minutes for the mouth to open. Then her mother took a breath, again very slowly. Then she started to speak, so slowly, that it seemed that the sentences contained only one word at a time.

"Lala," she said, "Because. It. Is. Not. Necesssssssary."

"Mommy, but everyone else is moving around all the time! Everyone is having fun all day! I watch them and I also want to have fun, like the other animals."

Apparently answering to this argument was very difficult for the mother, so she just remained silent and motionless.

***

A squirrel, a mouse, a duck and a turtle were sitting inside the squirrel's nest, eating lunch, when the squirrel said:

"Hey look, mouse, duck and turtle," he said, "I have got an idea."

"What idea is it, squirrel?" the other three animals asked him.

"As the sloths are so lazy, we have got to make them get up and move." The squirrel said. "They always hug the branch and stay that way forever. It's getting on my nerves."

"They're getting on my nerves, too," the mouse said, nodding.

"And on mine, too," added the duck and the turtle.

"That's right," said the squirrel, who was apparently their boss. "I have a plan. We must go and get on their nerves. Then they will come to their senses and most probably move."

"Squirrel, you are a genius!" The mouse exclaimed. "And why didn't we come up with that brilliant idea before?"

The squirrel smirked and got out of the nest, being followed by the mouse, duck and turtle. They approached the tree, where the sloths were hugging the branch, motionless as before.

"Hey, sloth," the squirrel said, looking up at the father sloth. "Why are you so lazy? Do you know that your name is Mr. Lazy?"

The other animals laughed. Father sloth looked like he didn't even care what they were saying. The other sloths also remained silent and carefree, except Sister Lala.

"Hey, that's my father, and don't you dare talk with him like that!" she said angrily.

"Hey, look, that sloth can actually move and speak!" the squirrel pointed to Sister Lala, in amazement.

"But her family members don't even care to move." The duck said.

"I am faster than you," the turtle said, giggling.

"I can even sing a song about you," the mouse said, turning to the sloths: "I'm so kind; I have made up a nice song especially for you!" The other animals applauded, and the mouse started singing:

You're so lazy and so dumb,
You can't even move your thumb,
You are hanging on the tree,
And look like it just can't be.

Everybody thinks you're dead,
We can't even make you mad,
Move your body, it's so easy,
Oh, we see, you're Mr. Lazy!

"That was so funny!" the duck said, laughing, but it seemed like the sloths didn't even hear it, except sister Lala.
"I think he doesn't even listen to us talking and singing!" The turtle said.
"I will punish you!" Sister Lala said. But she remained on the branch. She thought that it wasn't necessary to get down the branch. At least her mother had told her so earlier that day.
"We really want to see it," the animals said, laughing.

***

It was already evening. The sloths' family was still hanging onto the branches.
"Mommy, daddy, why did you stay silent and motionless when the squirrels came today?" Sister Lala asked.
As always, there was silence. Sister Lala shook her head in dismay.
"Daddy, but why didn't you say anything?!" she asked her father.

Slowly opening his mouth and taking in a deep breath, just like the mother sloth had done, the father sloth said as slowly as possible:

"Becauuuuse. It. Was. Not. Neccessssssssssary."

"This is ridiculous. It was necessary to talk back, daddy!" Sister Lala said angrily. "I must change this. I must make you behave like normal animals!"

"Sisssssster. Lala." Brother Bala said slowly, "You. Cannnnnnnot. Change. Us. Becauuuuuuuse. We. Are. Sloths."

"We'll see," Sister Lala said. "It depends on how big my wish is. And it's huge!"

Sister Lala got down the tree and started walking. It was a wonderful feeling. The movement was so pleasant, that Sister Lala kept walking and walking along the narrow path of the forest. Her family members didn't even bother to ask her where she was going. They stayed on the branch, looking carefree and unemotional.

Sister Lala had never walked along the forest path before, let alone at night. Everywhere there were shadows of trees, bushes, grass and flowers, moving under the moonlight. She was walking very slowly, turning around every second, and watching the nightlife in amazement and joy. Nearly all the animals were asleep. "I will break the stereotypes," she said to herself. "I will break all the stereotypes!"

Then she started singing:

Who said that sloths can't move or talk?
Who thought that we can't even walk?
Everything's wrong, everything's false,
We can run faster than the horse!

Tonight I set my mind to it,
The path is dark, it's dimly lit,
I want to find a magic way,
To change their attitude today.

CHAPTER 2. The Lizard and the Chameleon

Sister Lala was walking through the narrow path of the forest and singing under the moonlight. The night was peaceful. She was already tired and felt sleepy, as it was the first time that she had walked so much distance. Usually the farthest place she had ever walked was the tree a meter away from their current tree, where their whole family was living.

She found a bush and fell asleep under it. In her dreams her family members were walking, talking, laughing and behaving themselves normally. As well as she saw that the turtles, squirrels, mice and ducks were very friendly and never teased them again.

Happily waking up in the morning, she found a strange brown creature, sitting on her foot. Surprised, Sister Lala took that small creature carefully and placed it onto the green grass. Immediately the creature changed its color from brown to green.

"Hey, this is so interesting!" Sister Lala said to herself, "this creature changes colors! Let's try once more," she added, taking the creature and putting it onto a black rock. Immediately the creature changed its color from green to black. Then she put it onto a yellow leaf, and the creature turned yellow.

***

Amazed at her new discovery, Sister Lala was going to continue her experiments with the strange creature, but the creature started speaking.

"So, do you find it interesting that I change my colors?" the creature asked her, raising its eyebrows.

"Oh, yes!" Sister Lala asked, taken aback by the sudden question. "Who are you? You are such an amazing creature. I have never seen anyone changing their natural colors."

"My name is Chameleon," the creature said. "I change my colors easily. I acquire the color of the thing, that's nearest to me. And who're you?"

"Wow, you are such an interesting creature, Chameleon! And I am a sloth," she said. "My name is Sister Lala."

"A sloth?" the chameleon asked, turning blue, "but as far as I remember, my great-grandmother used to tell me and my siblings that the sloths were the laziest animals on the planet and they didn't move at all. She used to tell us that in fact the sloths were so lazy that they preferred to stay hungry for days, for the sake of staying still. But I see that you can walk and talk."

"Yes, Chameleon," Sister Lala said. "My family members are like that. They don't walk and talk. But we can move if we want. For example, I wanted to move and talk, and I was able to do both. And by the way, I like it so much! It's really enjoyable."

"Really?" the chameleon asked. "So, why did you want to move?"

"You know, I decided to break the stereotypes!" Sister Lala said. "My family members still think that for sloths it's most appropriate to be slow and lazy. Most probably they have heard it from their ancestors. But it's not very true!"

"I see. You are a very clever sloth." The chameleon said. "I like clever and brave animals." His color changed back to green, as he sat down onto the green grass again.

"Chameleon, why did you change your color into blue a few minutes ago?" Sister Lala asked him, "I don't think there's anything blue around you."

"Sometimes, when I am surprised, I turn blue," the chameleon said, laughing. "And sometimes when I worry, I turn blue again."

***

Sister Lala and the chameleon started walking together. It was such a magical feeling to have a friend. Sister Lala was happy and joyful. She felt that having a friend was the most beautiful thing in the world.

"Chameleon," she said, "how can I change my family members? Do you think there is a solution for it?"

"I don't know," the chameleon said, "but I have a friend, who knows many things. I think he can help you."

"Who is your friend, and where is he?" Sister Lala asked.

"He's a lizard, and he lives under the rocks of The Magical Rocks," the chameleon said.

"Magical rocks? What's that?" Sister Lala asked, surprised.

"It's a place, called The Magical Rocks." The chameleon said. "And my friend Lizard lives there."

"Why is it called The Magical Rocks?"

"Because they say that there exists a magical fountain that can heal." The chameleon said. "But I don't know exactly what it heals. We have to ask my friend Lizard about it."

***

They were already near The Magical Rocks.

"Pee-Puu-Paa-Pow!" the chameleon called, looking around.

"Chameleon, what are you doing?" Sister Lala asked.

"It's the lizard's name. I am calling him out." The chameleon said.

Sister Lala didn't have time to laugh because at that moment a green lizard appeared from under the rocks.

"Hello, Chameleon!" the lizard called, jumping onto the rocks and clapping his hands. "At last you came! I was wondering if you were ever going to make it to breakfast! I was going to prepare lunch and dinner, too, in case you showed up later. You are so slow, just like the sloths!"

Hearing the name sloth, Sister Lala stopped smiling. The chameleon said:

"Oh, Pee-Puu-Paa-Pow, if I am like a sloth, then it's a very good thing, because I have a best friend sloth, and she's kind of very fast, to keep it short. Her name is Sister Lala."

At that moment the lizard saw sister Lala for the first time. "Are you a sloth?" the lizard asked her, with wide-open eyes.

"Yes, I am. And as you see, I can walk and talk." Sister Lala said, "And in case you help me, the other sloths will also be able to behave like me!"

"Wow, this sloth can walk and talk! Nice to meet you, Sister Lala," the lizard said. "And I am Pee-Puu-Paa-Pow."

"Nice to meet you, too, Pipapupe, oh, sorry, I forgot your name," Sister Lala said, getting confused on the lizard's name. "I think it will be better if I call you Mr. Lizard. That way is easier."

The lizard laughed, and the chameleon turned blue. Then the chameleon said: "I think I will also call you Lizard, because your name confuses me, too."

***

"How can I help you?" the lizard asked Sister Lala.

"Mr. Lizard, My family members don't feel that they can move or speak, so they behave the way they do." Sister Lala said. "Apparently my parents have learned it from their ancestors, and my brother follows them, too. I want to find some solution, so that I will be able to explain to them that they will also enjoy being active."

"I see, I see," the lizard said. "Of course I will help you. Do you see that small fountain?" he said, pointing to a small fountain on their side.

"Yes, I do," sister Lala asked.

"It's called The Fountain of Stereotypes. It's magical!" he said. "Whoever drinks from this fountain, all his stereotypes are being broken."

"Wow! It's so interesting!" the chameleon exclaimed, immediately turning blue.

"It's so wonderful that I found this particular fountain when I need it the most!" sister Lily said, sounding very excited.

"You're welcome, you're welcome," the lizard said, bowing. "Now all you have to do is to bring them here, so that they will be able to drink from the fountain."

Sister Lala's happiness diminished. She became very sad. "But I can't bring them here." She said. "They won't come! They will not move. They just cling onto the tree branches like glue, and there's no way to make them move."

CHAPTER 3. The Magical Fountain

"Hmm, that's a difficult task, at least it seems like it," the lizard said. The chameleon nodded. Sister Lala looked at them helplessly and said:

"So what shall I do? Isn't there any way to solve this problem?"

"Sister Lala," the chameleon said, "maybe it would be easier to take the water to them instead of them coming here. That way we won't have to force them to move."

Sister Lala thought for a moment. "It looks like a good idea," she said, "but how will I transfer the water? In my hands?"

"Of course, no, Sister Lala," the lizard said, laughing.

"Then how?" Sister Lala asked, looking around, as if she could find a solution.

"Well, we can find something, a bucket or a basket. Then we can transfer the water in it," The lizard said, looking very clever.

"We must find something at first," Sister Lala said, "Mr. Lizard can you help us find something?"

"I'll try," the lizard said, disappearing into the bushes.

***

The lizard was rummaging in the nearby bushes for several minutes, and talking to itself: "Where is it? Oh, where is it? I remember that I have left it right here!"

Soon the lizard came back, bringing a small round rock, which had been naturally carved in, resembling a small and a very shallow saucepan.

"Here it is!" he said proudly.

"Oh, Mr. Lizard! Thank you so much! What would I have done if I didn't have such a clever friend as you?" Sister Lala exclaimed.

"You're welcome, you're welcome!" the lizard said again, bowing. "Now, let's start."

"But this is so small!" the chameleon said, looking at the saucepan and turning blue. "It can contain only a few drops of water!"

"A few drops are enough," the lizard said.

"In that case, I will do it," Sister Lala said. "I will use this saucepan and free my family from their bad stereotypes," and she held the saucepan under the water fountain. It got several drops of water in it. Sister Lala started walking slowly, back into the forest, along the path that she had come earlier that day. The lizard and the chameleon followed her joyfully.

"I hope this will work," Sister Lala said, sounding hopeful. Then she started singing:

The magical fountain is all that I need,
Its water is medicine, a wonderful thing,
I'm taking the water through the long forests,
I'll give it to my family members.

I've got some new friends, chameleon and lizard,
They help me a lot, outward and inward,
They give me advice; don't tease me at all,
They'll help me achieve my wonderful goal.

"Wow, this is such a nice song!" the chameleon said, turning blue.

"Yes, I liked especially the last four lines," the lizard said, looking very proud.

"It's because she's praising us, isn't it?" the chameleon said, nodding knowingly.

"Yeah," the lizard said.

***

They were halfway to the sloths' living place, when Sister Lala looked into the saucepan and shrieked:

"Oh, no, it's almost empty! There is so little water left! Almost all the water was spared! Oh, what shall I do?"

"Why?" the lizard asked, peeking into the saucepan.
"Oh, she's right," he added in a disappointed tone.
There were only a couple of drops left.
"Wow, it's really empty!" the chameleon said, instantly
turning blue. "I have no idea how to solve this
problem... Lizard, do you have any ideas? Sister Lala,
do you have?"
The lizard and Sister Lala shook their heads. The
animals stopped short, not knowing what to do.
"Let's go to the sloths' settlement, and think what to
do," Sister Lala suggested. "Maybe we can find a
solution there."
The lizard and the chameleon agreed and they
continued their way, more passively and hopelessly.
Sister Lala started to sing a song as they walked:

It's so wrong, and so confusing,
I thought it would be all right,
The water which I would be using,
Disappeared from the pot.

We are lost, sad and unhappy,
We do not know what to do,
When we fix it, I'll be happy,
And think my wish has come true.

They reached the place where the sloths were living.
As always, they were clinging onto the tree branches
and not even blinking their eyes.
"Mommy, daddy, Brother Bala!" Sister Lala called
them, "please look here. See my new friends!"
"It. Is. Not. Necessssssssssary." The father responded
so slowly, that the chameleon turned blue at once.

CHAPTER 4. Good Friends Are Precious

At that moment the squirrel, the duck, the mouse and the turtle appeared. They were coming towards the sloths. When they reached the tree and saw that one of the sloths was not on the branch, they got surprised and confused. They also saw that the active sloth wasn't alone: a chameleon and a lizard were standing by her side.

"Hey, what do I see?" the squirrel said, looking at Sister Lala.

"One of the sloths has decided to move around," the duck said.

"But why didn't the others follow you?" the mouse asked.

"Maybe they're slow, that's why?" The turtle said, laughing.

"Hey, who are you?" the lizard asked them, getting angry, while the chameleon turned blue.

"We are the squirrel, the mouse, the duck and the turtle. Can't you see it?" the squirrel said.

"Then why do you behave so badly? You'd better help us solve the problem," the chameleon said.

The animals fell silent. They were surprised that the chameleon was asking them for help, instead of making a fight.

"What kind of help can we provide?" the squirrel asked.

"And what kind of problem do you have?" the mouse added.

"This is Sister Lala, and she's a very active sloth," the lizard said, "she wants to convince her family members to be active, too, but they don't move. She thinks that it's a stereotype, which needs to be broken."

"Lizard has found a magical fountain, which cures all kinds of stereotypes," the chameleon said. "But we don't know how to make them drink it."
"We tried to bring the water here, but all that we had was this shallow plate, so we didn't manage to bring the water here." Sister Lala added. "The sloths won't agree to go with us to the magical fountain and drink the water there. And it's impossible to carry them to the fountain, because they are heavy."

***

The forest animals thought for a minute. They were proud that they were asked for help, and the sense of responsibility was big. Soon the squirrel said: "Thanks for trusting us and asking for help. To tell the truth, we didn't feel good for teasing you and your family."
"In fact," the duck added, "we were teasing because we wanted you to move. We felt bad that you were adhered to the brand all your lives."
"And it looks like our teasing helped you to get off the tree and live a normal life," the turtle said.
"But as the teasing didn't help the rest of your family, then maybe the teasing should be swapped with the magical water." The mouse added.
"Yes, I understand that you feel bad for the teasing," Sister Lala said. "But we have no idea how to bring the water here."
"Well, if we can't find any bucket, then maybe we must bring the water here by other means," the squirrel said, looking a bit confused. "Duck, you are the only one of us that has any knowledge about water. Maybe you will have any ideas?"
The duck said: "Well, I know that the water can flow."
"Flow?" The turtle asked.

"Hey, I also know something, which can be very important here, I think," the mouse said. "There are giant bamboos growing by the pond, and as the bamboos are hollow, we can make a pipe out of the bamboos, through which the water can flow!"

The chameleon turned blue instantly. The rest of the animals were silent.

"And how are we going to put together the bamboos so that we can make a long pipe?" the lizard asked. "The magical fountain is not near."

"I can find special herbs and plants that produce glue," the squirrel said. "It will not take much time. Sometimes I use that glue to repair my nest."

***

The duck showed everyone the place where the giant bamboos were growing, while the squirrel went to get the glue. All the animals started working on collecting as many bamboos as possible, so that the pipe would be long.

At last the squirrel came back and got surprised to see the pile of bamboos on the ground. The animals were waiting for the squirrel, so when he came with the glue, everyone started to work quickly to glue the bamboos together. As a result they made a very long pipe. Taking one of the ends, they started running towards the magical fountain, in order to attach it onto the fountain and get water flowing towards the sloths' tree. They were so excited and joyful, that the way seemed rather short and enjoyable.

At last they got to the fountain. All the animals tried to help Sister Lala to attach the end of the pipe onto the fountain. When they did it, they started running back as fast possible to see if the water had started flowing. As turtle was very slow and couldn't run, Sister Lala held the turtle in her hands.

They reached the sloths' tree, where the other end of the pipe was, and there it was! The water was flowing through the pipe and dripping off the other end. Jumping up and down with happiness, Sister Lala brought the end of the pipe towards her brother's mouth and the water started dripping right into his mouth. Of course he was too lazy to drink the water himself, but he had to swallow the water as it came trickling down. Immediately he got off the tree, saying: "I think I must move a little. I get tired of hugging the branch all the time."

"It worked! Brother Bala is moving and talking!" Sister Lala exclaimed, as the other animals applauded.

Then Sister Lala did the same with her mother and father, and they also started getting down the tree and stretching their spines and legs.

"It's so wonderful to walk and talk," her mother said.

"I don't understand why we never walked and talked before." Her father said. "Must be we were tired..."

"Hey, Lala," her brother said, "Let's play hide-and-seek!"

THE END

ABOUT AUTHOR

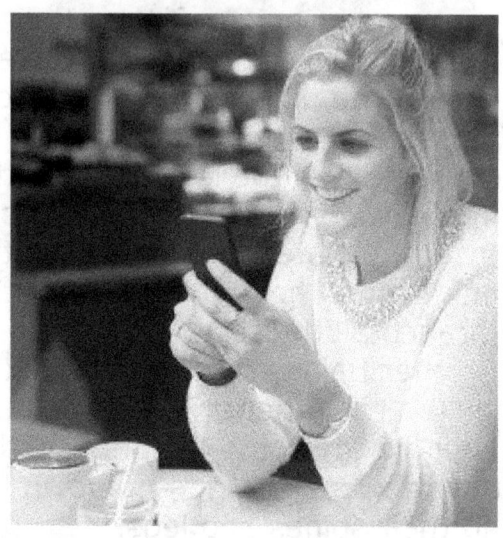

Nona J. Fairfax.

Nona J. Fairfax is an accomplished storybook author that has a strong passion for writing when it comes to improving the lives of children. She has a strong sense of pride for her work, and continues to thrive for a more universal world that keeps children and families in the foremost front of her mind. Her life's work includes writing children's books that help to improve the parent-child relationship, bedtime stories, and smaller pieces of art. When she is not busy writing about improving the lives of children.

MY BEST SELLER ON AMAZON

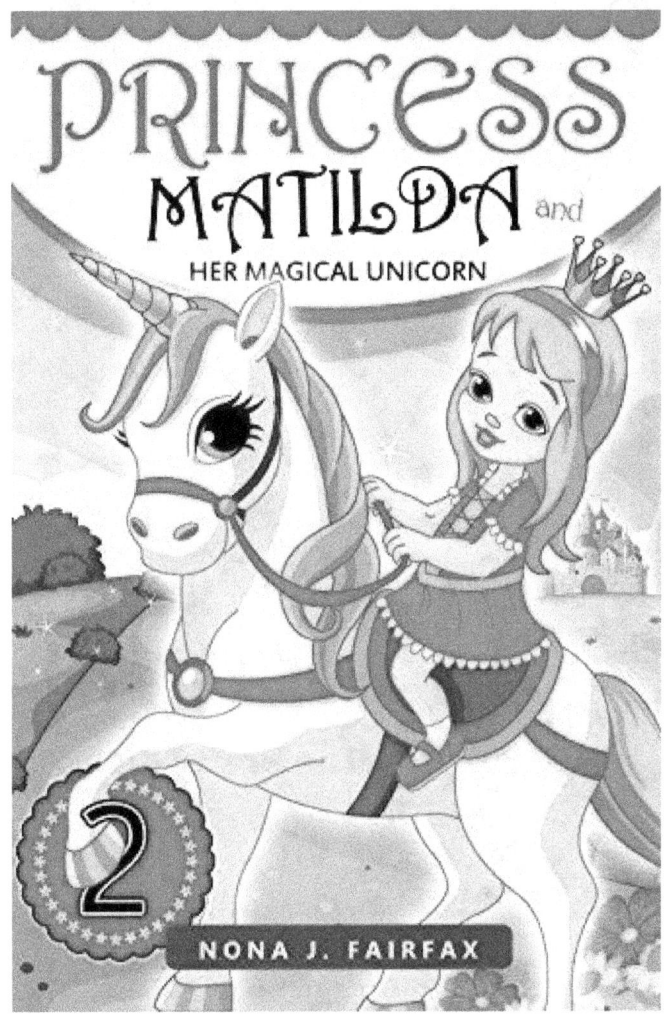

Download on:
www.amazon.com/dp/ B01GQKZYNK

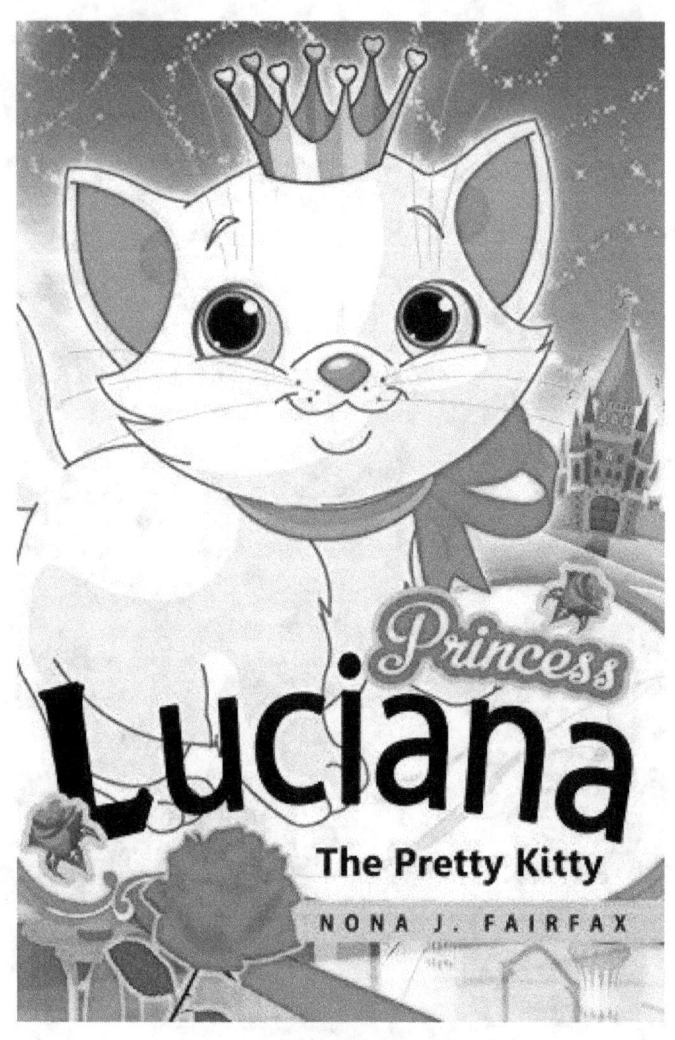

Download on:
www.amazon.com/dp/ B01GBJ65N4

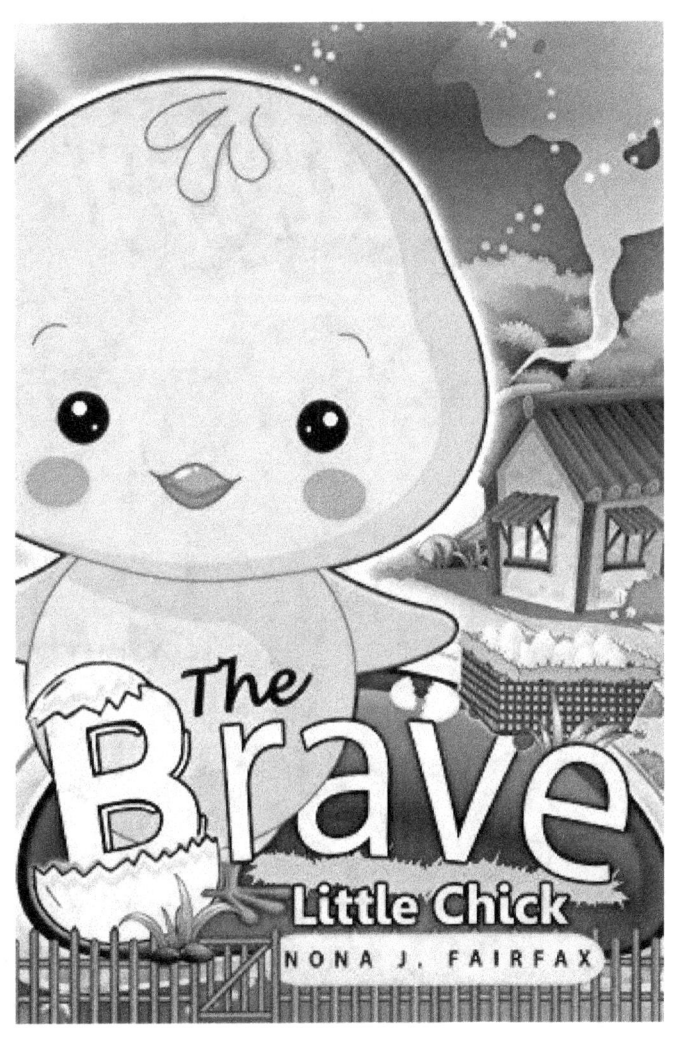

Download on:
www.amazon.com/dp/ B01JTIIZN2

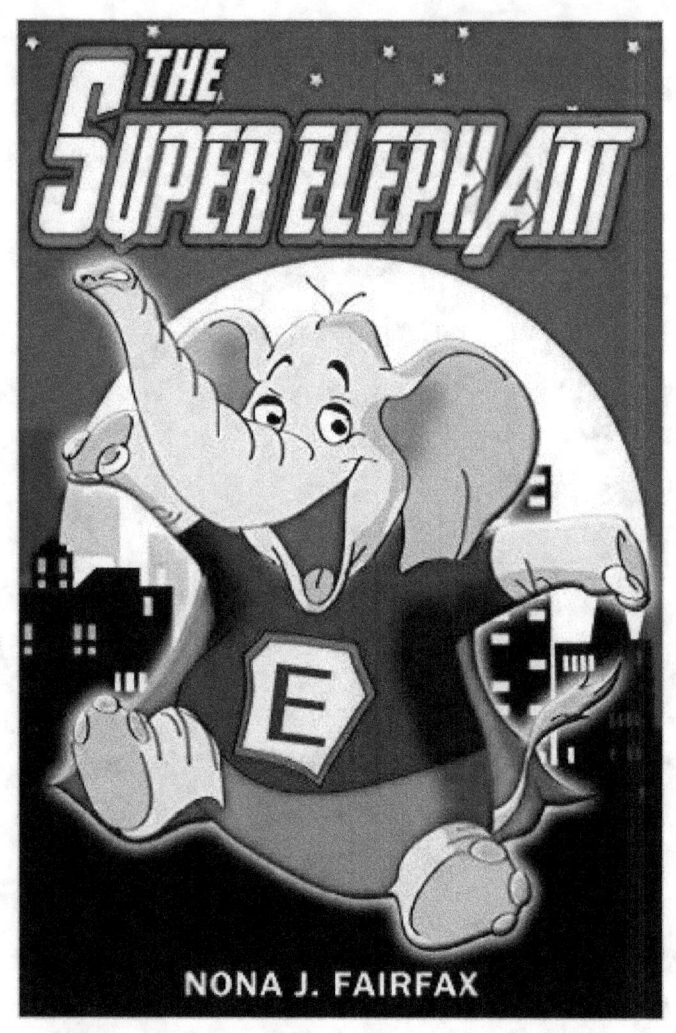

Download on:
www.amazon.com/dp/ B010EAB0JA

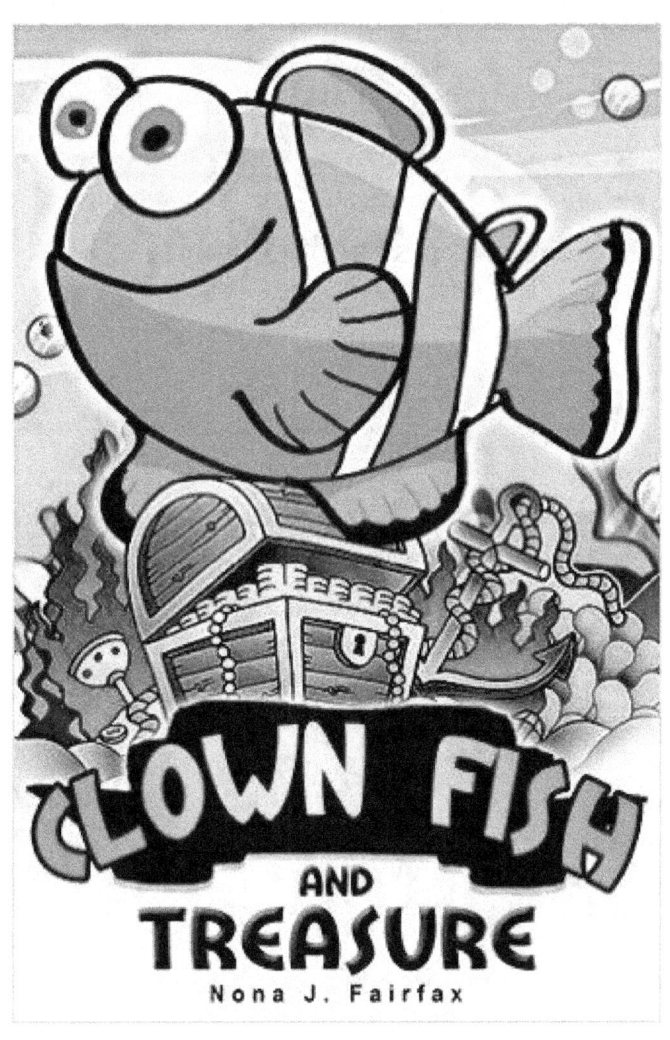

Download on:
www.amazon.com/dp/B010LP0TJU

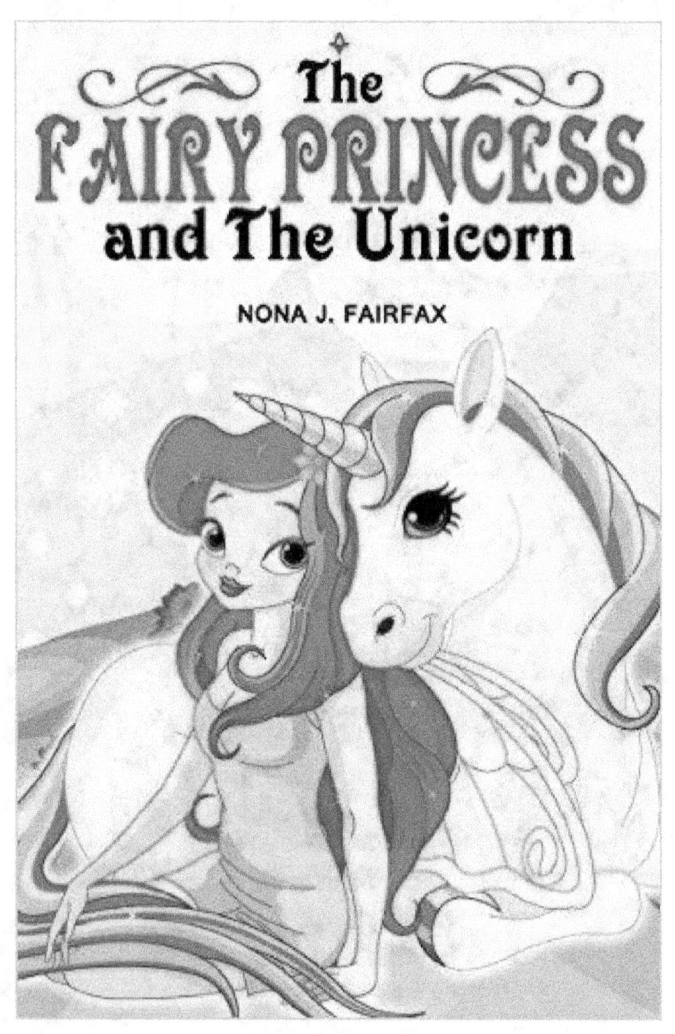

The
FAIRY PRINCESS
and The Unicorn

NONA J. FAIRFAX

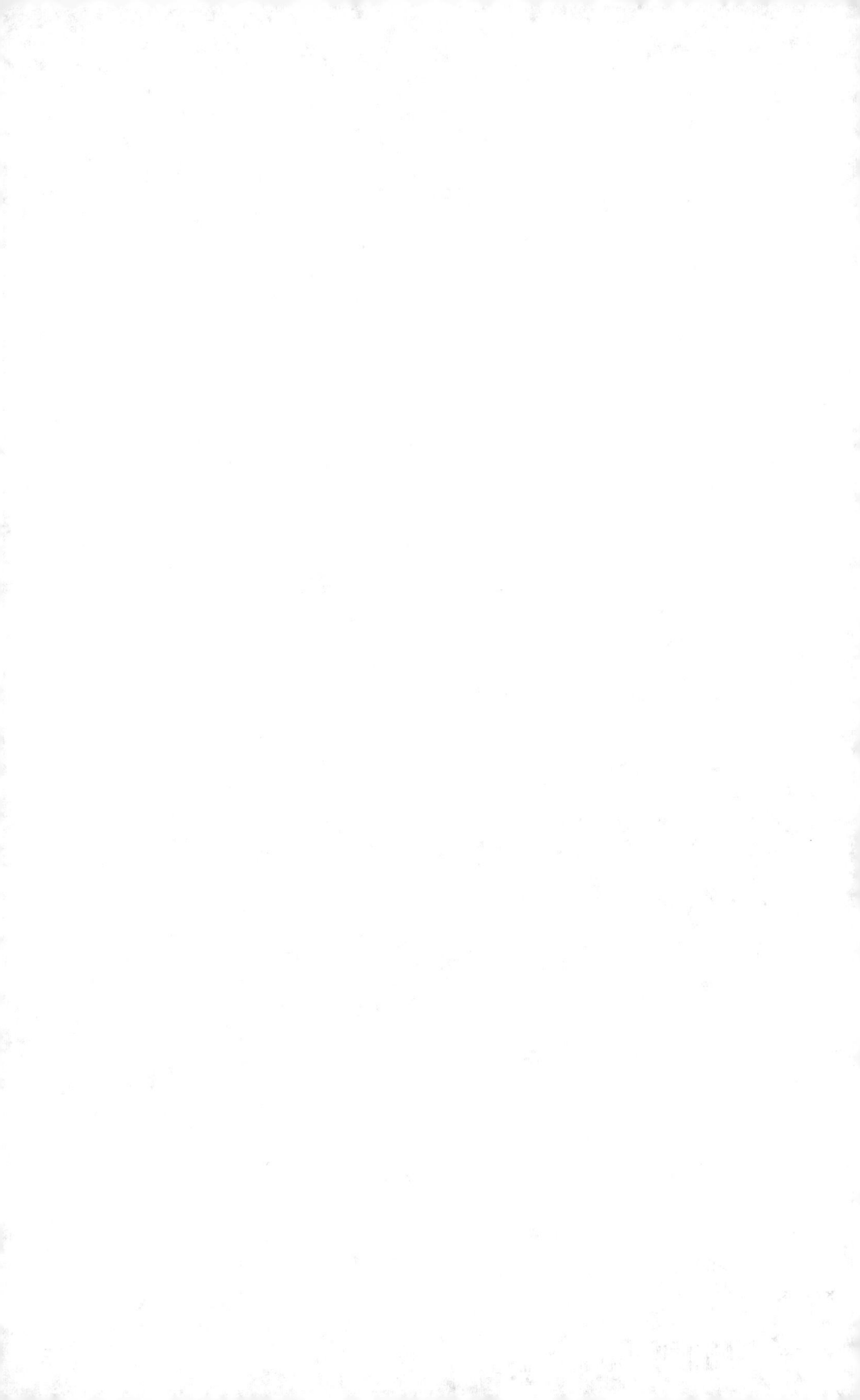

www.ingramcontent.com/pod-product-compliance
Lightning Source LLC
Chambersburg PA
CBHW071833200526
45169CB00018B/1425